Blood Run

Free Verse Play

ALLISON ADELLE HEDGE COKE descends from moundbuilders and is of Cherokee, Huron, Creek, French Canadian, Lorraine, Portuguese, English, Scot, and Irish ascendants. Raised in North Carolina, the Plains and Canada, she previously worked horses, fields, waters, and factories. The MacDowell Colony/Black Earth Institute Think Tank Fellow; professor, Institute of American Indian Arts (summer faculty, Naropa University); previously authored *Dog Road Woman* (poetry, Coffee House Press) which received the American Book Award, *Off-Season City Pipe* (poetry, Coffee House Press); and *Rock, Ghost, Willow, Deer* (memoir, U.NE.).

Blood Run

Free Verse Play

EARTHWORKS BY
ALLISON ADELLE HEDGE COKE

SALT

CAMBRIDGE

PUBLISHED BY SALT PUBLISHING
PO Box 937, Great Wilbraham, Cambridge PDO CB1 5JX United Kingdom

© Allison Adelle Hedge Coke, 2006

First published 2006

Printed and bound in the United Kingdom by Lightning Source

Typeset in Swift 9.5 / 13

ISBN-10 1 84471 266 4 paperback
ISBN-13 978 1 84471 266 3 paperback

TB

1 3 5 7 9 8 6 4 2

This volume is dedicated
In Memory of the Original Citizens alongside the Big Sioux River
In the former City known today as Blood Run

*   *   *   *   *   *   *

And to everyone working to preserve and protect
Sacred sites, sites of Indigenous civilizations,
Humanity, humaneness, humanness—
The lands, plants, creatures, people, life.

This volume is dedicated to the mound builders of many nations and to
the memory of trade between Pan-American Indigenous peoples with the
prayer that one day the routes, camaraderie, will flow free between all
again without impediments by oppressive restrictions or regimes.

Contents

Introduction

by Margaret Noori

Miisko Bmaapto

What defines a place with blood invoked in her name? How does blood run—in cycles, perhaps, from one life into another, masked by a ghostly powder chipped one speck at a time from the silken side of a granite boulder? Stones, like bones, speak with an elemental voice, an ethereal timeless hum at a pitch some never recognize, but resonant enough to guide the souls of others. Allison Hedge Coke challenges readers to attune themselves to this place, Blood Run. She teaches us that this is a place on earth exactly like no other and yet very much like many other sacred sites. She teaches us, this place, Blood Run.

It has a name now, given by the nation that surrounds it—Blood Run National Historic Landmark Site. It has a location on the maps made by today's mapmakers, located on both sides of the Big Sioux River in western Lyon County, Iowa and eastern Lincoln County, South Dakota, south of Gitchie Manitou State Park, approximately $\frac{1}{4}$ mile south of county road A18. It has a size measured by the mathematics of modern man. The main portion of the site extends over at least 650 acres. Judging from a few projectile points recovered from the surface, the site is "pre-historic," as defined by historians of today. It is said the site extends back in time to as early as 8,505 years ago. Archaeological evidence suggests that the heaviest years of use may have been between 1675 and 1705 A.D., when it was occupied by as many as 10,000 individuals, trading and interacting in social and ceremonial activities, sharing an Oneota cultural tradition. These are odd parameters. Would the Oneota consider their ancestors "pre-historic" or merely the mothers and fathers of mothers and fathers of mothers and fathers on into eternity? Would the population be counted only in living souls? What would they make of the separation between "B.C." and "A.D."? And best of all, what would someone who speaks any of the Algonquian languages think of a location point "south of Gitchie Manitou," literally a place just "south of God?" Sacred sites throughout the country embody similar cultural issues. They stand in contrast to contemporary ways of knowing and understanding this life and the one that follows.

The words in this book were put down by Allison Hedge Coke, but they speak of something more than one person alone can own or contain. These poems are personal, intimate and yet meant for all eternity and all ears. They are bits quarried from another academy, a school of holistic philosophy that encompasses both the past and the present. This book is not a delicate act of nature worship or revelation of shamanic secrets. These are poems in which the stones, the trees, and the community speak clearly about life, industriousness, work, patience, mortality and birth. These are stories of cupmarks in granite, bends in the river, gently-shaped earthenware, harvested beans, fish bones, bison hides . . . carefully laid remains . . . invisible souls perceived.

This is a book of accusation and promise. Blood Run is unique among Oneota sites because of the documented 176 mounds. Approximately 80 mounds are still visible on the surface. These mounds were engineered of carefully selected stone and soil, tightly packed, designed to resist the intrusion of the ages. Some mounds are still over six feet high and measure 80 feet in diameter, solemn sentinels into the future. Stories tell of an earthen serpent, but it may have been destroyed by railroad construction. These mounds are holy places that have been violated, excavated, desecrated and described in archaeological reports.

As farmers, developers, and state boards of tourism debate what to do with Blood Run, they ignore what Blood Run can do for them. They note that to preserve the entire Blood Run site and its 'visual environment' would require protection of approximately 2,340 acres. So in 1987 the Iowa State Historical Society, in cooperation with the Iowa Natural Heritage Foundation, purchased 230 acres of the site. How is it that we can choose to remember and honor one tenth of her, this place called Blood Run? Plans for the site include prairie restoration, building an interpretive center and creating a trail system. It is a step too small but better than no step at all. If we honor the past and listen to its voices in a way not clouded by our own times and troubles, we may learn to see beyond the present. The message of Blood Run is as simple and as complicated as that. There are ancestors and there are descendants and there are those who recognize the rights of both and those who continue steal from either one as needed. The poems of Blood Run are cupmarks, small indentations on the surface of our souls, invocations that cannot be ignored. Allison says it all when she writes, "no human should dismantle prayer." A prayer, words offered to someone, someplace, something beyond our comprehension should not be interrupted. By writing this book, she begins the mending of a rent in the fabric of sacred spaces on earth.

MARGARET NOORI

Foreword

Previous to European colonization and conquest efforts and some might say despite of it, trade flourished between Indigenous peoples of the Americas for perhaps as long as time earmarked humankind. Evidence of continual trade throughout the Western Hemisphere, including art, symbolic items, and practical tools, was well cached in the multitude of mound cities puckering vast portions of this continent, some still incredibly existing after decades of continual and intentional desecration, disfigurement, and dismantling by looters, grave robbers and Manifest Destiny driven anti-eco agriculturalists. Though surely there were times of upheaval and/or harmonious discord for Indigenous Americans, these long-developed relations also ensured survival during eras of doubt, for traditional Native rural and urban livelihood.

Traditionally, when a separate nation of Indigenous people needed to take refuge or safe harbor, a host tribe might accept wampum, or other symbolic gift, and adopt them as a sister/brother nation then provide protection for them while helping them to sustain themselves and providing humanitarian aid. This was an archetypal practice even amid former foes and enemies of war (including prisoners of war). Thus the likelihood of peace prevailed and most nations enjoyed the security of blanket protection, aid and assistance from related peoples, whether by blood or agreement. In so much, nations that enjoyed helping one another sustain themselves also traded amongst each other and engaged in trade relationships with numerous additional nations outside these pacts.

Throughways, whether by river or beaten path, were so extensive it has been said that practically all roadways in the hemisphere, including the now far overdeveloped United States, previously served these trading and adoptive relationships. Likewise, language systems were shaped and evolved from core, or root, languages to allow ease in trade; including the distinguished trade language spoken in the southeastern area of what is today called the United States: Mobilian. Such systems ensured survival of individual nations equally as well as confederated, regional and the broader Indigenous Americas.

Blood Run is such a place, one of significant trade, once a great city.

In a time where so much devastation is occurring to Indigenous peoples, with impending danger in Colombia and many other Latin American countries; the continent environmentally endangered from the Arctic Circle down; where coral reefs are dying and polar bear drowning; where power mongers consider drilling through glaciers in Chile; deforest to conquer; where the largest human threat is commercialization of oil, coal, ore; where the Nukak are today facing what Indigenous people faced at this mound city less than three hundred years ago; this memory is a significant reminder of these civilizations at their peak and how critically important it is to preserve cultures, climates, architectural ruins, and sacred sites as they exist. It is imperative.

ALLISON ADELLE HEDGE COKE

Author Note

Oneota designates an Indigenous building culture on the Midwest Prairie Peninsula, sometimes the term is translated as a large group of peoples; other times translated to Place of a Rock. It is noted (State of Iowa Parks Bureau) as Algonquian, having been lifted from a former name of the Upper Iowa River.

In the scope of humanity, the beginning of the 18th century is not long ago. Eastern Indigenous Nations were already entering into treaty with England at the time maps and census counts were first being made of this heavily populated and thriving prairie city by French traders and Voyagers passing through. Yet, in the genocidal oppression of millions of Indigenous peoples, the very cities which only pre-dated European resettlement, or destruction, have been classified as ancient regardless of population periods.

Technically, in this case, Blood Run qualifies as both. The settlement dates back over 8,500 years ago and was definitely dwelled within until the encroachment. Artisans here created copper works, pottery, stoneworks, and great earthworks built for burial, civic, ceremonial and symbolic purposes.

Upon the first European encounters, as many as 400 mounds existed in upward to 2300 acres. 276 mounds were surveyed in 1883 over 1,200 acres. Later only 176 were mapped still visible. Due mostly to looting and physical removal, and later to cropping directly on top of the mounds, now perhaps less than 80, thoroughly diminished, mounds remain. The desecration by non-Natives has been immense and immensely unnecessary.

Strangely, though Native people were living in the city when European people arrived and traded with them, and despite the fact that Natives were still using the site during the development of the United States, Euro-Americans, for the most part, refused to believe that the same Indigenous people populating the region built the mounds. Publications dating from the 1800s to only a short time ago written by Euro-North Americans declared the mounds were built by a people who had come and gone. Unfortunately, for the early scholars, they missed any opportunity they had of actually researching the history accurately by ignoring the facts (and people) in front of them in earlier days and were relatively late in understanding the local Aboriginal myths are not only metaphorical moral story, but actual history of literal places and lives belonging to these very places. Such as this place, Blood Run.

This manuscript is dedicated to the original peoples of Blood Run site area, including: Ho-Chunk, Otoe, Ioway, Kansa, Omaha, Missouri, Quapaw, Osage, Ponca, Arikara, Dakota and Cheyenne Nations.

Blood Run

For Travis

I

Dawning

Before Next Dawning

Before Next Dawning's vermillion rise,   for tens of hundreds of
        years, life was
as it was,   life itself,   for thousands upon thousands,
across Horizon where plumed,   feathered ones danced
        skyward,
tiny ones crawled   beneath long grass,   raised by summer
        heat.
Upon Earth's surface thundered   thousands upon thousands;
        hooves, feet.
Doves warbled, crickets chirped, elk whistled.   Sun rose, fell

In the midst, a trading place,   settlement,
six cultures, bands, tribes,   ten thousand People,   families
        entwined.
This was a place where a traveler might rest,   take water, elk
        meat, catfish,
delight in warm company after weariness.   A place of peace,
        place of Wáwan.

Marking worldly occurrence,   as all People do,
structures, from gathered earth hauled in baskets,
strategically placed, forming designs—animal, geometric—rose
        reverent.
As People passed, significantly honored with mounds, knolls
of their own,   they became part of this landscape   Immortal.

Medicine boulders, from past settlement,   carried, implements
        sharpened,
etched in accordance, cosmology principles, changes—
        Rendering fine pink granite
dust to make red, or ghost-white face paint for mourning, and
        on so.

The People lived as they were told—hunting, fishing, farming—
worked with one another as cities do.
Prayed together and alone,   as People tend to do.
The government steadily worked for common good of all
        citizens
as all governments are supposed to. Eventually a cosmopolis,
        where
they lived, prospered, sometimes traveling River
to other settlements for trade, to import, export goods.
Sometimes   settling in, relishing afternoon Sun—easy.
This is the way it was and The People
were sure would always be.

Stories began circulating
a coming of a new kind.
Stories common as combing hair,
preparing food, water,   ritual.
Keeping track, counting experience,
instruction, education, social event,
as Story existed around entire Mother Earth. But,
these Stories foretold   terror, unthinkable, whiskered
beasts of men who thought nothing of putting end to life—
woman, child—The People. Strange men
without families   who came in night,
siccing war dogs, sounding monstrous weaponry,
killing without touching, without arrow, spear.
At a time when to touch an enemy
gave greater valor than ending life.

The Stories told of Strangers coming,   hordes in
boats arriving upon Land's watery eastern edge.
Disasters drifting their journeys' wake.
Once Story relayed entire families sleeping peacefully
waiting for dawn, incinerated in Night   by the new kind.

Eagle bone whistlers sounded prayers, warnings.
Whirling blackbirds, heckling crows considered insect clouds
rising from peculiar domestics—alarming.

There was proof.   Strange blankets,
with saturated color, weave not of prairies,
plains,   not of buffalo hair, nor dog hair,
nor any plant ever worked here before.
These blankets preceded the coming   through trade
amongst all The People living upon Turtle Shell
compromising the Northern body, this Hemisphere spanning
from the Arctic to Antarctic where some hundred
million People were already so securely home, before this
        dawning.

First,   when blankets came,
The People were mesmerized, soon coveted   daily wear.
Presage foretold soon revealed through odd illness.
Not like any infirmity had ever blistered
upon The People until this time.
Plagues of great magnitudes,   where

thousands upon thousands succumbed,   relentless wrath.

Marks fell upon the earth—the Strangers' powers.
Power of death without touch,
without seeing odd instruments   throwing fiery,
pellets into Human Beings from distance away.
Power without resounding instruments.
A grave mark fresh upon Earth.
A scar, revealing itself through papules, vesicles,   pustules,
umblication, crusting—pockmarking People.   Killing power.
No roots, herbs, no bear grease, nor deer medicines proved
effective to fight its course. Souls released like Spring
        cottonwood billowing, samaras soaring—

Disease unleashed upon   This World from Variola blankets
traded upon contact, sealed trunk hoarded,   strategically
removed from bodies, from victims in The Lands Across Waters
far, far away.   Brought here, they wrote, to make colonization
easy task. Lain over, like laying strange spread, making dead.
      Task proven
in other escapades of Stranger mankind.   Germ warfares.
Not the first ever practiced   on Mother Earth's face,
yet the first collusion here and   The People who had always
      been
soon were almost lost. Those surviving vowed to
remember what had been before,
ensure their children's children never forget
hosts of ancestors preceding them, building their world.

This is world history. This gorgeous settlement
nettled with bluestem, red grass—Blood Run.
Pitted pink granite testament to thriving culture
of time before New Dawn,   before new disease,
new ways,   iron blades, guns, money—
Before sacred horse returned, carried them seasonally further
      away from home.
Before lands were overrun in Strangers, settling in, erasing,
      erasing.
Before time when world erupted in natural life interruption.
Somehow, miraculously, this place still boulders Horizon.
Yes, this is a story of Blood Run, of sudden
regional mound culture departure. It is a story.

Facing renewed plague fears,   newly imagined
deliberate unleashing of Smallpox,   let us not
erase what has happened here before.   Let us
remember   men, women, children, sacred infants
who succumbed to such disease   spread by

approaching new mankind,
who certainly   appeared terroristic
upon thick grasses,   natural prairies, plains.   Upon
original inhabitants as hide counts trace.

Let us count, how often we witness sacred sites demolished,
toppled during yet another overthrow.   Hear my plea.
We silently witness desecration,   many cultures'
sacred sites, east, just as the world   witnesses gravel pits,
golf courses, housing, saloons, cafes erected   upon Indigenous
        Peoples' graves
without regard to Great Grandmothers, Great Grandfathers
who sleep here in this land   puckered with soil
carried in many, many wound,   coiled, woven baskets,
by dozens and dozens of hands working in unison
for common good   in building earthworks, effigy,
community civic sculpture, structure,   safe barrier bound by
earth, taking in the bones of The People   upon their untimely
        passing.

Sun pulls blue up from Darkening Land,
raises the lid each dawn over these same ruins,
this great civilization   of time ago,
Over the ageless prairie   glistening river, streams.
It is in this dawning   consciousness is raised.   A chance.
An age for man to now reflect respectfully
upon another man's glory.   Yet,
testament in danger still, monstrous machines,
bulldozing scars upon soil,
lifting the earth's very skin up,
barring her bones, bones
of her People   for raking,   then smothering her
breath   with concrete, brick, mortar—

Never more allowing her   to freely breathe.

May she breathe again.
May she breathe.

May the revealed find refuge.
May the revealed find peace.
May she breathe.
May she breathe again.

May the revealed find delivery.
May the revealed find hope
May she breathe again.
May she breathe.

May the revealed find hope.
May the revealed find delivery
May she breathe.
May she breathe again.

May the revealed find peace.
May the revealed find refuge.
May she breathe again.
May she breathe.

May she breathe.
May she breathe again.

II
Origin

River

I remember the living
building earthworks all along my banks,

for eons before the Changeling.

First Story, then pressure.
Pox narrowly preceding his dreadfulness.

His presence, reckless squander.

My People began to row, then walk,
then ride, to maintain lifeblood, sustenance,
elsewhere upon the mother.   In their leaving,

leaving me offerings to care for
those they had to leave behind.

The others, Changeling summoned,
mostly respected only themselves.

Not generations lain out before them.
Not sculptural works, nor practical.
Not mare's tails above, nor horsetail within me.

Yet dare claim me, harnessed, bridled,
as if I were not betrothed.

When from my wellspring
to my journey's foot

my cherished rest along me still,
for their attendance, my watchful pace—devoted.

Clan Sister

I have come to pray
I have come to sing
to dance before you

Call you to   rise
again, to enormity
behind pulsars.
To the universe.
To Stars.

I remember when we
laid upon our mother,
followed starry lead
each night here.

We welcomed
their motion,
twinkle.
Crossed worlds
under, above   mirrored
in eight-point stars.

Now, I pierce earth with
hawk feathers
upright, standing on
quill point, barb.

Line the old paths,
paths of spiritualness.
Guide you here
as do the stars
each crossing.

Though I lead you here,
allow you privy,
dare not exploit entry.

Memory

Wrapped in doe albino
heads held as if racked fully.
Eyes peeking through
two-fingered split space.

Sentries stand nightly,
strong in summer starlight,
among chest-high tall grass,

Surrounded in big bluestem,
little bluestem, switchgrass,
fever leaf, fever stem, mint,
butterfly weed, breathing root,
goldenrod, pasque flower,
deer medicine purple-bloomed—
positioned amid plenty.

Above mounded ridge,
shouldering circular planet.
Securing Horizon's distant edges,
ledges premising reason, discord.

Scanning the entire universe
for movement,
for pathways of planets,
for arrivals from the east.

For those arriving.

Horizon

Turtle-headed guards linger on entryways.

Stone circles sign space,
await return of those who complete
with care, with pine-poled hide,
fully beaded, quilled,
circumference symbolically painted.

Or, bark lodge roofs held taut,
grounded in river rock ellipses.

Earth lodges perpetually lingering, caches
filled with paintbrush, roots, curative tea,
Corn, Squash, Beans, sustaining sisters—Sunflower.

Allies here laid stones,
designed eagles, thunderbirds, falcons, serpents
on prairie; patterned dance, stone, clay, copper.

Though treasured lost lie here entombed,
in near distance hollows belie scaffolding
once raised to usher neighboring
loved ones on final journeys home.

To the place that is in everything,
spark existing here,
where I wait unflinching,
spanning relations   of all you know,
knowing dawnings come, go—
knowing.

The Mounds

Rising from earth-black, rich-fresh soil
lifted, hauled for multitudes in woven baskets
piled one on top of another, again, again, laid down
upon overlaying ground base, allowing drainage, for long-term care,
until we appear as small, circular, sloping hills to untrained eyes beholding.

Here, the earth is sanctified, sacrament caressed.
Created by cultural duty,   by love for The People.
Prepared to preserve proper burial of loved,   cherished.
Of those who lived in honor, in respect for Mother Earth, they
rose from, returned to remain encased in our earthly wombs sheltered.

Lain precise in accordance; constellation rise, cyclic phenomena, lunar cycle,
solar event; in the manner of being positioned relevant to all that was—will be.
Measured by line, multidimensional, geometrical design, envisioned, embraced, made form
from rope lines calculating paths, fiery loved ones guiding us here in this world from far beyond.

Ceremonial Mound

Altars raised from flatland
where The People might together praise
what holds the unending universe intact.

Platforms allow dignity admired, extolled.
Positioning measure far above mortal reach.

Higher than common ground
Favorable to kindred unearthly.

Climb upon my table, my bone plate.
From here, you can touch the clouds.
From here clouds embrace.

You can diagram the phases
of Sun, Moon from my ledges.

People, climb me together,
eyes to Sky; feet on Earth.

When elevated, even bold break.
Safer sending sentinels who know their purpose.

The lifting may swell loose humility, place.
Touch clouds, witness, breathe, behold, leave offerings.

Return to The People, humbled.
In this way. In this way.

Burial Mound

Keeper of Stories—
legacies of Life.

Solutions to unknowns
within my venter.

No one has known me
for these hundred years,

yet those who know me
know my form Immortal.

I, dwell sculpted
loved, by a People of Creation

Wise men, blessed children, mothers of stars
slumber in perpetuum, the seat of my mass.

Morning Star

So quickshot across Sky Vault.
they think me imagined.
My shawl fringes Earth
each dawn before Sun breaks Horizon.

Call to me each passing.
In the fleeting dawn await,
I will float you through
appearing peril.

Through me the world awakens.

Sun

They raised their faces
four times each day, night.

Sky's seat, when my stride was high,
welcome upon their crowns.

As in Toqua, Chunkey throws
confirmed rival worth beneath me.

They brought triumph.
I, warm embrace.

Surrounding themselves
with domestic companions.

As I, my dogs, parhelic anthelion,
loyal to me as I am devoted.

A true surrogate revealing
Mystery's ardency
in manifest physical form.

Through me all live.
My gesture, yellow, red
—abundance, purity.

Dog

Woman's companion, helper,
I lug, pull everything she would bear.

Trusted with infant, meal bowl, case.
My only wish, her pleasure.

Wag, to signal all well in the world.
Nuzzle, whenever she fall saddened.

Give myself to medicinal purpose.
Satisfy her need—hunger.

Whatever whim of wander, impulse
she sees fit,   to care her deliverance, I heed.

Shhh, something's on wind.
Though I remain steady, ruff raised,

I fear for her.

Starwood

They strike me four times,
heave me upon faithful shoulders,
hoist me true,
each time they join to dance.

I mark the way of water,
show stars in each
snap—limb, twig—

I am life.
I am life.
Touch Earth, bring Stars.

Merge this world and the next,
dance before me.

Corn

They took deer, elk scapula, scraped soil
just enough to loosen my path.

Drove a planting peg,
turned, held to one side
as I dropped dried
into wet earth,

gave goodness,
pollen, meal, kernel,

made them over each time
remembered in prayer.

Dance for me.
There will be plenty
here for you
again, again.

Raise your faces,
shoulders skyward,
knees give, straighten,
feet gentle touch—

You can figure the phases of the moon
by my sprouting tassels.

Redwing Blackbird

Feet firmly perch
thinnest stalks, reeds, bulrush.
Until all at once, they attend my
female form, streaked throat, brownness.

Three fly equidistant
around me, flashing.
Each, in turn, calls territorial
trills, beckons ok-a-li, ok-a-li!

Spreads his wings, extends
inner muscle quivering red
epaulet bands uniquely bolden.

Turn away each suitor,
mind myself my audience.
Select another to consider,
He in turn quiver thrills.

Leave for insects.
Perhaps one male follows.
Maybe a few brood of young,
line summertime.

Silver Maple samaras
wing wind, spread clusters
along with mine, renewing Prairie.

As summer closes, I leave
dragonflies, damselflies, butterflies,
mosquitoes, moths, spiders, crickets for

grain, seed, Sunflower;
join thousands to flock Sky—
grackles, blackbirds, cowbirds,   starlings—
Swarming like distant smoke clouds, rising.

Sunflower

Multitudes facing Sun,   our
rough, broad extremities near touching.

Simultaneously attending
to receive warm embrace.

To welcome flower, water
swells behind my broad head.

At night bows gently resting;
preparing to greet new morn, to

raise me full glory to greet
strengthening summit—daily heliotropism.

Motor cells, pulvinus, flex stem
below bud until flower opens

my yellow shawl fringe,
exposes seed, welcomes bee,

forever-facing forward until my passing.

Trade Story from the south speaks our
venerated image, Inca Sun.

My seed plenishes.

Moon

My children were buried 'neath altitude,
within masses of earth as their sisters mourned them
with painted faces resembling my spirit full.

They sang for them to enter into realms
upon light of Milky Way, upon the ells,
annexes of a thousand fluttering crow.

The white owls' heads wound round and back
as Spirit instructed The People how to circumvent further loss.
It was this way for time before coming tide.

Before stomping of milkweed, darkthroat shooting star.
Trampling of prairie chicken nest eggs, downy phlox,
loess cratering—plow, till, dozer, crane—
Before tampering Blackbird's grain to poison.

I peel off slivers from this ball
rolling across my set domain
remembering all those who look to me
for guidance, advice, revelations.

Blue Star

In cold, I dangle in west,
pendant, above charred sunset, lightning.

My shining brightens frosty exhalation.
My balance, perpetual precision.

Tattooed upon chosen.

I bring purpose, mean you well.
Sparkle brilliance into valor when

upon Horizon a shifting phase
appears, beyond fine earthly balance.

Look to me when change requires courage.
My face bears all will, stability.

North Star

By me multitudes thread earthly blanket,
set their paths to come, go,
weave their ways nightly.

My glistening steadies destinies, homelands.

Though our positions fluctuate,
far longer timeline, seemingly still.

In their day, upon mounds, gazers divined, trailed
flashing phenomena, approximated eons,
cleared space with deer mandible sickles,
raised spherical jars, shell-tamped pottery, punctate,
engraved serpents, hawk wings to commemorate lower, upper.

One handle for each grasp, chevron marked.
Observing, measuring, guarding throughout Night.

When the moon manifested just so, word arrived.
In unison, in step, they raised, offered, crushed to potsherd.
Precise to drainage needs in new moundings, lain like
        constellations—
paid tribute to our crossings.

Like supernova appendages, seven fiery points,
painted, etched in hills to the west,
through us they mapped star roads,
corn meal pathways, expansions, explosions.

Night stars, dayblind continuing ever on.

Both will remain drifting precession, long
after this world runs its course.

The Mounds

Each basketful they bore
a thousand steps or more,   prayed each stride,
as they piled earth upon earth, to form our bodies.

Whispering praises to everything that is, will always be—

For millennia we made model
each rise, fall; Sun, Moon,   Immortal.
Reflecting honored pathways; grandmothers, grandfathers.

As we grew, their love for us flourished.
Our appearance made resemble pitched earth.
With every prayerful glance, acknowledgments ascended.
With every ascension a place on earth mirrored constellations, eternals.

With each layer, came credence; reverence,
nothing, no one then, would venture destroy purpose
our holy graceful place upon which you now stand, dignified.

Somewhere along the way, the world went inside out,
yielding, unfolding, to tools crafted to scrape unbearably ransomed.
In this turning, all we have come to hold, now exists in jeopardy.

Snake Mound

Present invisibility
need not concern.

My weight remains
heavy upon this land.

Winding,
weaving, incurve,

mouth undone,
for egg swallow.

Though my body
suffered sacrifice
to railway fill,

my vision bears
all even still.

Be not fooled.
Be not fooled.

I will appear again.
Sinuous, I am.

Esoterica

My presence, ancestral blood,
lets prayers glide spirit path.
Instrument moulded,
lifted in quietly soulful moments,
in solitude, company of ghosts.

II.

Near creek waters,
only Dogwood rivals me.
Under my robe, near skins
provide blood, smoke,
spark between Creator, Creation.
I am sacrament for some nearby.

III.

Take me in your mouth
tuck me into cheek pockets,
or in between teeth, lip.
Bite occasionally.
Let my bitter flow doctor
throe, heal ferment.

Muskrats follow advice,
instruct you.   They prevail
while you anguish
in vicissitude that comes.

IV.

Ever I reach upward
lace green into ever blue.

My sprigs spark life, popping
upon stones glowing red-white

waiting with their stone mouths
to speak only truth,

as you often wish to
wear honor upon your own lips.

Through me this is possible.
When wind blows, I sustain.

V.

Being female,
I flower much fuller,
bring relief during moons
bearing conception.

My brother
extends himself
higher than sole reach,
lending himself
to you for ritual.

Together, we bless—even now—
in our offering,
gray smoke rising.

Take tenderness, sprigs,
over crown, brow.
Over, through
rough hands for solace.

VI.

Perfectly square lengths
char smoldering.
Incense offering infants
sleep, dreams, peace.

VII.

My figure sacrosanct,
Counted reverence.

Clan Sister

There are deer here.
I can feel them.
Antler firm, pelt soft
lingering close by.

Ghost Deer.
Albino white.
The entire herd
a miracle.

Wondrous revelations
occur rarely.
Once a lifetime.
Here, twenty-four

snuggle treelines
wintertime
camouflaged.
Sisters of mine.

Deer

In the old,
when seekers came,
we gave ourselves freely
each season rolling.

Shared our soul, our store, robe,
with every good heart—uniting
with mindful People through our own suffering.

Watched them approach us robed as ourselves.
Took to two legs to move among them freely.
Sometimes advisory, sometimes exchanging.

Gave our tongue, so they could speak
in the language of our brethren clan.
Know our insight, dreams, as brothers, sisters.

Now, we dash, flee silently, leap
tawny, white, from grasses, bush, treelines,
upon arousal of thunderous echo banging.

There has been no peace in these lands
since the dead have been threatened,
landscape unjustly encountered.

There is no peace tonight.
We must take cover, move.

Beaver

When this dam goes another will follow.
No amount of rainfall deters me from
what I am borne to do.

That tree, the sculptured one
was only practice.
I spooled the bottom in three days
upon the fourth I took its limbs.

All wood was meant mine
so long as I have reason.
What reason has he
to take ample,
make scarce?

Buffalo

Wallowing where once
glaciers swallowed ferns,

churned stem, skeleton,
civilization confirmation,

wrung all headlong impractical
to depths beneath today.

It was always as was
time, time ago.

Rushing prairie grass
so thick, we created roads
for your kind to meander.

Follow me to highest ridge
hurl me all four hooves over
I will sustain you in life
through my own passing.

Replenish me still
through song, prayer.
My return is closer
than most dreams dare.

Fox

Silver, red run, black legged,
thick-tailed, sure-footed, we
swiftly dance upon earth
divine—harmony honors us.

Pelt generous as our gifting.

It is we they imitate
instilling rules, order.
Perhaps we still wait their call.
Stake ourselves here   daring.

Memory

Wearing white mourning paint
powdered from pink granite
weathered light as crusted snow.
For prayer, song, story—life.

Laying out our world in shapings, come Cohokia.
Planting three sisters—Corn, Squash, Beans—
circling each mound in retrospect—dancing, drumming.

Marking our bird-print presence.
Buffalo marks on Pipestone Tablets,
on boulder stone,
on the belly of the earth,
on every raised ridge,
seasonal hide,   come winter.

Fortification? Hardly from human. Mere walls honor
cyclic astral events, bring whereabouts, announce our city's
welcoming—honor patrons—Puma, Thunder, Snake!

Ho-Chunk, Missouria, Ioway, Otoe, Quapaw began
Omaha, Ponca, Kansa, Osage joined. The Honga. Soon
Arikara, Cheyenne, Dakota as well,   negotiating trade,
        camaraderie,   or not.

Millennia ago we initiated young here.
Until strangeness, disease, danger encroached upon us.

Ten thousand strong then, this city
invoking ceremony, ceremonial chance,
feasts filling significant days, nights.

The winds winding each of the hundreds of
hills raised, revered by man
under glory.

Cupped Boulder

From me lives were earmarked
blazed, blessed, eternized.

From me medicine
saved cherished lives.

From me nights were honored, stones
carried, days glorified, faces decorated.

From me Thunderbird, rain,
greatly appeased.

From me thousands wore
striped markings, holy.

From me The People
walked west to water while mourning.

From me they rose
together to certify the living and the dead.

Pipestone Tablets

Birds bless ages,
track daily presence, part, whole.
Outlaying movements, momentum,
recording ritual, rudimentary toil.

Buffalo markings trace comings, goings upon these slabs
a language according to symbolic design, by man
reveals written accounts of the time before Next Dawning,
reveals our presence, patterning, purpose—

What ill could wish such knowledge obliterated?
What has come disguised as human beings?
What work has Stranger's will? What repulsion?

His seed, seven strong, will return us to our own People.
All tests,   generations bear.
All temporary,   beyond balance, grace.
We record balance, restore, give grace, prove tenure—

We will replenish.

III

Intrusions

The Tree at Eminija Mounds

My limbs outstretched
once again as in my human life.

I stand before you
naked and without shame

without contempt
or hate.

Without need for explanation
nor compromise.

Here, in this life,
I am free to stand upon this earth.

Holding memory from a thousand years ago
of a People once flourishing

on this same ground
once sustaining life,

a holy innocent, cut quick,
whose greatest wish was to return

without frail flesh
of common man.

Here, I stand before you.
Here, I stand.

Burial Mound

It's tenuous releasing
what belongs below us.
Memory thrives here.

Sometimes, in early spring,
when white ash bud fresh green,
waters fall from gentle above, they shift.

Perhaps remembering Buffalo—days spent
gathering saplings, black and golden eagles,
one crow, one swan, buffalo skin, shell disk, kettle—

From oak-cedar woodlands, bur oak savannah,
floodplains, onto mixed grass, prickly-peared flats,

young would dash for fresh heart, twenty tongues.

    They gathered.   .

I do my best to shelter, keep them.

Sometimes,   perhaps remembering,
from my tilled base, barely protecting gatherings

a finger reaches out to test the temperature.

Ghosts

With Redwinged Blackbird grace,
we raise red grass as we pass over
    field, hill, meadow.
The swirl, our motion
    wobbles leaves,
        causes scarlet bee blossom,
pimpernel, tall grass to swing
    as if they run.

We swirl loose dust, white, red,
fine powder lifts, sparks
in afternoon sunlight.

This familiar rustle
    has been known since
        time in this world began.

Leave us amaranth, goosefoot,
lamb's quarters, knotweed, anise,
Ree tobacco if you meander long.

Some of us have skeletons nearby.

Skeletons

What the physical embraced ties us here,
longing for what was familiar.
Since silence overcame this sanctuary,
sounds flute solely for those who have ears.

She who hears, come know us.
With stillness, walk among us.
Without malice, note our presence.
Glad-hearted remember us, our glory.
In this time, malevolence must leave this place empty-handed,
                              unnoticed now.

This way we subsist.
Once numerous, now our scalp locks, occipital bones,
merely satisfy seekers, irreverent in a world
we should not know.

Jesuit

What lies here must be pagan,
but what pagan lies were old?
Could it be that Memory
rules this land enriched with soul?

What roams here in the twilight?
What harkens here twofold?
What essence was it made of
when the centuries turned cold?

Some fine day Blue Cloud Abbey,
will invest our mission role.
To honor Benedicton
pray, work, study, soul!

Clan Sister

When you see me
in the distance
you believe me
speckled brown
wide-eyed,
pawing earth
for fresh shoot.
When I have foot
not hoof
am upright,
bipedal,
since my early days.
Do not be afraid.
I will bring
my Sister for
The People to survive.
She will surrender her robe
for blessing.
When Meadow Lark
comes calling know
it is I in nearby.

Squatters

We are farmers, settling.
We have right to work
lands in untamed wilderness
rife with beasts best done away
with blasphemous symbols—Snakes!

What good is this to savages
who have no learned appreciation
of possibility of a ripened, bountiful place?

They know no possibility, no progress, no personal greed!

They should be grateful we've brought
civilization onto this merciless barren flat.
That the greatly merciful Royal Historian of Oz
soon calls for their timely ending.

If they cannot be tamed,
we should do no less than answer
their deviling wizards' ways while we still can.

Netting Passenger Pigeon; blasting buffalo; exterminating
bear, wolf, lion;   poisoning coyote, prairie dog,
cottontail, jackrabbit, gopher, vole—Blackbird—
it takes a ridding to cleanse for our purposes.

One nuisance as useless as the next.
Cavalry comes rescue, whenever we give call.

Manifest Destiny guarantees our rights.
We are the chosen   self-appointed lordly hosts.

In a hundred years, all of this will belong to the till.
All of this taken under, razed, obliterated—done with!
It is God's will as we know him.
It is our destiny, this providence.

The Mounds

In our day
we were many,
so many landscape
appeared pleated, puckered.

Our cityscape stellar—splendid.
Design mirroring universe—divine.
Spirit in all that is, all that was, will be—relative.

In time before, time ago, we rose so high, eagles
Peregrine Falcons, red tail hawks smiled upon us while soaring Sun.

Our People created us, cared for us, provided the most
esteemed existence in intricate esoteric societies, thus in return we cradled them.

Tractor

It is my duty to plow, my work
to turn earth to something
my master thinks precious.
Least the weary rise.
Let it not be said I
judged this domain
anything but worthy of
my own steely blades.
You were nothing to conquer
nor contend.
I was proud to take you
under, rid you of your
presence here.
Hold no grudge to me.
You should be grateful
I have freed you
from all that mounding
they lay upon you.
Worship me, know my truth.

Horizon

Red grass appears
rames between bothersome
brome brought by encroachers
long ago.

Thistle shoved
each purity aside
that for one brief eternity
held her face east
as Sun passed over.

Longer still ago,
builders made this
landscape ripen
with each basketful
blessing flat land
with beauty,

with commemoration,
celebration of life,
procession,
natural occurrence—

Death deserves
her place of permanence
though soul belongs to
swirling cosmos,
Holy Road unbridled.

The Mounds

We are the love of man honoring mystery.
We hold him close inside our deepest neo-grottoes.

Since the beginning we have longed for him, come
near us once again. We were not formed to be forgotten.

We were raised to protect, well guard him, lay him down to rest.
Our reason, his sanctuary, now in the midst of those who've conceived new history.

Who've taken these lands without return, without recompense.
Through us   hopes, visions, dreams, notions of his time are made known.

Skeletons

All that is good is with us—
remains in subtle dusk,
holds the base of lifetimes.
We belong here. Let us be.

Do not unsettle us.
Do not bring harm, nor further journey.
We have finished with this world,
have returned to it.

Until there is dust we must remain
settled here where we were lain.
Our People labored for this honoring
no human should dismantle prayer.

Looters

We come in day searching, calculating what may in night.
Surely it is our right to take what was abandoned.

Badgers edge out what we cannot reach.
Nothing is sacred in this world. Nothing.
Artifacts? They're not using them anyway.
What practical good are they to the dead?
Illogical sentiment, braceleted wrist bones.

We have journeyed here for this specific find, knowing
there is no reward waiting those without initiative.
Our fingers, files, picks, brush finish off intended fortune.

Thereby gravel pits do not thrill us,
only remind us of the trace we left behind.

Burial Mound

My seed coat meant for sheltering. chambers choate.
Though now my beauty furrowed, furled so
I can scarcely shield the remains of my People,
nurture their blooming spirits for anthesis.

Their heritage seed below at Macy, in Omaha—
They speak to me, from both sides,
turnip hole; still breathing.
Each needing antithesis to fare well through me.

So lamentable, what was!

I was a fine, broad hull, tremendous testa.
From far distance, rivaling hills
lain like kernelled landscapes, ideal body.
Before the novices came chiseling to ruins.

I, endure wrath of the till
bludgeoning of benighted.

Take pity upon me! I appeal.
Without my womb, they but dust.

Early Anthro

Surely bones can tell.

I haven't time to talk to
those who speak in riddles.
They haven't earned my trust,
proven their scholarship valid—evidence!

Even so, bones just do not lie.

To interpret their story uniquely,
transliteration—personal truth!

Translation, form fit genre,
for we who name the world
in our own image.
For we.

We'd be dead before permitted.

Get on with it, I say.
Antediluvian, antetype!

We'll stir the dead with tibia.
Rouse them in fervent flute anthem.
Nothing ventured; nothing breached.

River

Each road here
was worked over deer tracks,
bull buffalo furrows.
All led to and from my private ways,
providing imports for life.

Trade occurred here.
Marketplaces from time before silver,
before coin, from time
where People bartered for
wares they worked and then some.

A white shell rose
from the west where
red stone facing back
was waiting.
Each offering gifts
with their presence.

To this day tooled stone
still holds Memory.
The shell long ago
gave great cluster—
Today brittles in the cache
of a collector's drawers
splintered.

Looters

Iron rails backed shoofly into her central mounds,
for easy freight car loading—heart-beaded beauty,
double-sided, quilling, leather, copper, stone, skull—
Railways reaped grave bounty, sacred sentiment,
as if they were gathering grain.

We culminated enough handmade treasure,
revenue haul, on coupled rolling stock,
our hats beavered, collars ermined, minked fine.

First set out back east, then west, in boxcars,
well cars, freight wagons filled
flush to line museums coast to coast.

Whatever didn't dwell our desire we fed
crushers, hoppers, ballast dumps—
Dakota rail sides, roadsides, still
wear scattered, intermingled remains.

Pulverizers petal shoulders for our treading.
Our glory? We made a fortune manifest.
Because of our duty, skulls, skeletons, line pathways,
assist White students schooling in handling of the body.

Transit makes proper use of the forgotten.
No medicinal breakthroughs happen without proofs.
Evidence gave testimony, attestation in our collection.

Our devotion presented confirmation with little sacrifice.
In the beginning, our load, five acres square loot.
What today appears a valley, then tombed hills.

Our children's children hoard the rest.
Heirlooms from tycoon follies.
To appease the homesteads,
we sprinkled some back around—baited them.

Clan Sister

They curse themselves
each time they approach this place.
The sentiment of animus
winds round puffed heads intruding.

No rest will come to those who
take the troves this place embraced.
No rest, no peace, no honor
follows those who rob these stores.
The chevrons in their pockets still able.

In their blindness,
they presume concocting Story
of wild men, wild women,
our home as wilderness,
denigrates realness
elevates stature.   Yet,
as nature is our mother,
they imprecate themselves
alone.

River will come for them.
She only rests till time
needs her to bathe, wash over.

Without offerings
She will come swollen,
snatch them up like pollen,
disperse, dispense, derogate.

Wet earth profuse once more.

Early Interpreter

It is sculpted prairie;
mystery left by vanished,
so very long ago.

Let us now begin to tug away
European thistle bent on choking
pure Native growth.

Let us confuse the Looters,
do let children come to know,

but let the White men tell the Stories,
descendent Native must comply.

In the end, our message weighs
much heavier than gathered dusts—blood, bones.

The Mounds

Interpreter, socialite,
doesn't hear us like the others.
Merely recites as she's been told.
Instructed to carry out measure
without recognizing balance, blood stopper.

She chances here, there poking, prodding.
As if our bareness nay embarrass
enough to consider our still held pride.

Long ago, we were well-cloaked, monument raised.
Our parameters shunted by boulder, stones form laid.

How did it happen ones like her have come here?
Did medicine abandon true human kind?

If so, quickly appease.
Lay offerings night, day.

We sorely await Reclaiming.

Stone Snake Effigy

Before ignorance
my length was modeled
for protection,
sacred presence.

Presenting myself fully so long.

Now these stones,   still mark
glorious envisioned
being I once was.

What is now considered miles
once stretched by rope-lengths.

Walk along my length made
considering what is done, will be.

What is necessary surely remains so,
regardless of hands, or hearts of man.

My purpose thus exists among needs
of the world to this very day.

Recognize me to free thyself.

Memory

When disease rode trade blankets
wove way across oceans, rivers,
my People reeled. So many crossed
into the next world, my fullness ruptured,
poured as sores upon then-tainted blistered skin.

It was too much for Memory, to bear.

Since time ago, slowly erased all
eye could see, truth held
within my reaches for falcons'
sure vision. It is in these vaults
time, place, I exist even today.
In the end, all will dissipate, join me.

Horizon

Though thick with many,
all over the world,
People remain alone.

Often, pasts of those
who traveled on becomes
something Memory
may not sustain.

Dissolving along
perceived parameters,
sensible tangents—
illusory.

Head in rain,
feet deep earth,
my pointal plane
of existence reigns.

Drenches imagination,
saturating glory
seven color
deception.

Though, truth be known,
my complexity
rests on axes,
altared.

Clan Sister

No matter how long
He lasts here,
do not tell Stranger
what Memory knows.

Tertiary tendant,
he will take truth,
scorn meaning

until ashes fall around us
like detritus winds
across mound tops, loess ridge,

like hail pummeling
surface of creek,
river below,

where green darners,
black-winged damselflies
keep constant watch, wary.

Katydids, crickets,
cicadas revel secret song—
congenital memory.

Primary comprehension,
blood memory will emerge, engage.

Some of our loved ones'
children's children will

return here some day—speak for us!
Until then—

Do not tell. Do not tell.
Do not whisper.

Skeletons

If they had wellness
they would live
here below us
along River still.

If the waters kept
their enemy at bay,
we would have great
company even now.

What was bustle
is now returned to still.
Who will leave us
offerings to tide us over?

Horizon

I belie myself to today's travelers.

Hundreds of years before,
beyond former city life bustling
in this now quiet place,

where Earth alone
retains this earthwork practice,
though their descendents do survive,

proof all made,
made eternal through me,
through my witness,
here within my peripheral span.

Over the ledges of the world
legacy does still flourish.

The Mounds

In this posture
we've seen the rise,
and leaving of nations.
We've seen ten-thousands
wearing soft-skinned formalities,
harmoniously live in prosody with Water,
Earth, Sun, Moon, Stellae, Cosmos with all their
essences gleaming for most brilliant millennia, or so.

We've seen
passages—livelihoods—
scattering doe, bird, larger herds.
We've seen hustle,   Chunkey play,
fast comings, deadly unspeakable enemies,
chomping teeth devouring us—take all we've known.
Here, in this wintering of our old world, this harboring—time—
we've become another marker, one who must bear mortal memory.

IV

Portend

The Tree at Eminija Mounds

My reaches long,   lift,
stretch above   in prayer,
below extend
          to touch earth   *in prayer.*

On right,
          dipping lightly, waving fringe westward.
On left,
          glad spirit returns to me, running.

In this form,
upriver from focal dwelling,
freed to open myself amply.

In this fashion
          rooted, liberated,
                    acumen leafed.
In this shape,
          prolific.

Sheathed now, fervent, burly,
Shielded, fixed, ingrained in terra firma,
Rooted below, outstretched above—open—

What in last life failed me,
in this life liberates.

Ghosts

When all the doghair, squirreltail, foxtail,
porcupine, buffalo, pony grasses run
impression strummed,
along slopes, gradient rise—

When Mullein presses low,
red willow limbs quiver, whirlwinds shiver,
release silver-spotted skippers,
monarchs,   white butterflies
take to wing, to firmament—

lifting miracle commotion,
phenomena now we.

In translucency of leaves,
overcast sun, rolling,
lightening, shadowing   breadth of green—

In this acuity, this keenness
Insight pronounces utterances
not unlike prophesy.

For those who heed, prefigure, perceive.
For those who distinguish
modern from manifest,
in everything all familiar.

We will have beckoned you to return to us,
return our skeletal remains to shelter here,
return our longing.

Then, in quiet whispering,
momentary stillness reveals.

Prairie Horizons

Where wind blows, ice chills forty below full winter,
early springtime releases waters from faraway melt.
Marking air with moisture, ground with possibility.
It trickles relief where glaciers once roamed rock over,
flood-cut stone clean as glaze,
welling rivers, streams, swelling swirls slipping wile.

Here, this place resumes lusciousness.
Until as it was, returns dashing with fury,
unshackled liberation, burgeoning—
Walleye leaping from the rushing
as if to spare themselves scores on
Sioux quartzite quick edge,   leaving breathing haven,
for pummeling pivot, bulleting from cerulean to blue, into
butterfly wingroom shock, red rock surrounded space.

Those seeing merely horizontal beauty
miss the crevices, creases, puckers, plunk, pluck—
my bounty pleasures,   loess straddles,   amid all motion
in between my edged banks cut keen into distant sky.

From all of this,   I once witnessed Strangers
bring iron, brass, glass, guns, horses (how they once cliff-
        jumped them).
Sixty million I'd mourned Dawn Horse! Meso, mio, pliohippus—
larger equus, loping here from a million to at least till ten
        thousand years ago.

Leaving here during global warming past; natural, not climate
        interrupt now dawned.
Horses, sacred, prophesied to return, my People did greet with
        praise, glyphed prints.

All withers changed, then carried my People further and further
      away each season,
until the intruders quarreled use, tenure, possession—
pushed, then brutally edged them aside.

That's the thing with ledges.
Beyond the edge of the universe, may be only beyond this single
      prairie line.

Skeleton

It's clatter
teeth on teeth,
mandible on mandible,
bone relaxed into bone
that makes you fearful,
yet the same rests
within you
as exists to form me.
Release me from
collections.
Free me to free thyself.
It's clatter,
teeth on teeth
bone on bone
come fearful.

Clan Sister

In hallowed grounds
seldom seen species
endure beyond tendering.

Our wealth abounds
within what we preserve.

It is our guardianship,
serpentine defense,
sentinel sheltering humble.

Sacred is the place
where gentle thrive.

Snake curls us here,
providing method.
Ever offering cures, spirit,
induced in ghostly coppers.

Melding ore, knife
to ornament,
to cast her image,
adorning adoration.

She remakes herself
in each made thing.

Winding our wrists, arms,
dancesteps, dreams.
Returning always
one way for fate.

Her lifespan eternal, star roads high.
Her inimitable presence stippled,
patterning our world.
She River, we revere.

Skeletons

Just yesterday some of us returned home.
Away from archeological scholar filings,
home where we should have always lain.
Just yesterday before, we were still live.

In the time passed while life developed
our framework, fully cultivated casing,
while structure of our statures discerned,

we were perceived as one with The People,
now possess mere remnants of all we were,
souls passed, relative to all surround.

We still stand the test, uphold each,
every essential instrument of life as it exists.
Still relishing essences, tastes, hours of humankind,
await opportunity to sleep, to sleep, to sleep, to sleep.

The Mounds

Civic, ceremonial, elegant effigy—Snake—
our purposes funerary, fundamental, immaculate.

Until Sons of Orpheus, fools of fortune,
looters, anthros, squatters—their tractors, rakes—
altered, removed on superiority-driven raids.

When the animals leave this place,
now without protective honorary sculpture.
When River returns with her greatest force.

When flora, fauna will themselves back,
here where we all began ago, long for.
When our People return, to the place
offerings kept free, balanced, hallowed,

when The Reclaiming comes to pass,
all will know our great wombed hollows,
the stores of Story safely put by.
All will come to truth.

We allowed you entry to gain
your sentiment, consideration.
When you leave here take with you,
only what with you came.

What has come to pass, though troubling, still
will bring you comfort deep in night.

We were meant to make matters meaningful.
You, who know no glory, must know you
will lie down just as those here have done.

For you, learning has begun.
Let your mind be mindful.

Memory

Shhh, crickets are singing.
What takes to wing now folds.
All that we consist of must be made implicit, ghosts.

Corn has the hardest task.
the squatters have used you
since setting down, bearing arms.
Now orchestrating genomes, rushing
your beauty, your seed. Plowing
what remains of us to ruin, in your name.
Yet, innocent, nourishing you remain.
In the night you are forgiven, made over,
dew-kissed, visited. Our dearest loved one
they keep captive. One day you will join us.

My Peoples.   North Star, Blue Star, Morning Star will
give you direction, strength, cleansing.
All around you makes medicine, purified.
Sun, Moon over all each turning
Raise your faces, touch lightly—dance.

Cupped Boulder, Pipestone Tablets, ceramics
testify to your glory, to splendor on this riverway,
to spiritually sentient ways of being,
to beauty, brilliance—magnificent.

Buffalo have come and gone, with us bountied.
They suffered deathly warrant wrath of those needing control.
Tortured, they laid scattered, skinned bare, rotting
until the bone collectors came for them, too.
Yet just as our children's children have little ones
seeking us again from the places they do dwell nearby,
they too, are returning to proximity for sacred sustenance.

In the meanwhile, every beaver, silver fox, deer, dog,
will know us. For now, for earthly presence nigh.

Epilogue

Clan Sister

Redwinged Blackbird.
Sunflower bids her, her suitors,
each growing season
since planting began.

In our day, we shared enough
to return plenty.
Nurture to nurture
our ensuring way.

If feeding overcame them,
a scare to watch over.

Her seasonal feeding
ever unwelcome now.

Since Stranger reduced
our glory to cash crop,
his crazed impulse
set him to premeditate
murder, six million redwings.

Shooting, DRC1339
Starlicide into rice
sacred food upon waters, turned poison for

Blackbird, redwing, yellow-headed,
grackle, Great Black-backed Gull,
pigeon, crow, raven, magpie
Baird's Sparrow, Chestnut-collared Longspur

and all that might
unknowingly take of them:
heron, kingfisher, cormorant,
hawk, eagle, vulture, owl.

For food they've favored
for eons; for eating Sunflowers
grown for sales, wild bird seed,
for Redwinged Blackbird,
for eating pre-purchase.

As if Blackbird has pockets cash-lined.

When the Animals Leave This Place

Underneath ice caps, once glacial peaks
deer, elk, vixen begin to ascend.
Free creatures camouflaged as
waves and waves receding far

from plains pulling

upward slopes and faraway snow dusted mountains.
On spotted and clear cut hills robbed of fir,
high above wheat tapestried valleys, flood plains
up where headwaters reside.

Droplets pound, listen.

Hoofed and pawed mammals
pawing and hoofing themselves up, up.
Along rivers dammed by chocolate beavers,
trailed by salamanders—mud puppies.

Plunging through currents,
        above concrete and steel man-made barriers

these populations of plains, prairies, forests flee
in such frenzy, popping splash dance,
pillaging cattail zones, lashing lily pads—
the breath of life in muddy ponds, still lakes.

Liquid beads slide on windshield glass

along cracked and shattered pane,
spider-like with webs and prisms.
"Look, there, the rainbow
touched the ground both ends down!"

Full arch, seven colors showered, heed

what Indigenous know, why long ago,
they said no one belongs here, surrounding them,
that this land was meant to be wet with waters nearby
not fertile to crops and domestic graze.

The old ones said,

"When the animals leave this place
 the waters will come again.
This power is beyond the strength of man.
 The river will return with its greatest force."

No one can stop her.
          She was meant to be this way.
                    Snakes in honor, do not intrude.

The rainbow tied with red and green like
that on petal rose, though only momentarily.
Colors disappear like print photographs fade.
They mix with charcoal surrounding.

A flurry of fowl follow

like strands, maidenhair falls,
from blackened clouds above
swarming inward
covering the basin and raising sky.

Darkness hangs over

the hills appear as black water crests,
blackness varying shades.
The sun is somewhere farther than the farthest ridge.
Main gravel crossroads and back back roads

slicken to mud, clay.
    Turtles creep along rising banks, snapping jowls.

Frogs chug throaty songs.
The frogs only part of immense choir
heralding the downpour, the falling oceans.
Over the train trestle, suspension bridge with

current so slick everything slides off in sheets.

Among rotten stumps in black bass ponds,
somewhere catfish reel in fins and crawl,
walking whiskers to higher waters.
Waters above, below

the choir calling it forth.

Brightly plumed jays and dull brown-headed cowbirds
fly as if hung in one place like pinwheels.
They dance toward the rain crest,
the approaching storm

beckoning, inviting, summoning.

A single sparrow sings the stroke of rain
past the strength of sunlight.
The frog chorus sings refrain,
melody drumming thunder,

evoked by beasts and water creatures wanting their homes.
Wanting to return to clearings and streams where ash, or
white birch woods rise,   tower over,
quaking aspen stand against
storm shown veils—sheeting rains crossing

pasture, meadow, hills, mountain.
Sounds erupt.
Gathering clouds converge, push,
pull, push, pull forcing lightning

back and forth shaping
windy, sculptured swans, mallard ducks, and giants
from stratocumulus media.
As if they are a living cloud chamber,
As if they exist only in the heavens.

Air swells with dampness.
        It has begun.

Acknowledgments

A South Dakota Artist Fellowship and a National Endowment for the Humanities Distinguished Visiting Professor appointment at Hartwick College generously supported this work. The South Dakota State Library, *Parthenon West Review*, *New Medicines*, *Ploughshares*, *The World*, *Abiko Quarterly*, *The Café Review*, *Political Affairs Magazine*, and Denison University have published versions of work included in this volume.

Once, a snake mound effigy of a mile and a quarter length, much like the worldwide lauded Snake Mound in Ohio State, existed in this very place—Blood Run. The railroad used it for fill dirt. Train tracks were lain right up into the main mound area for eager looters to sell back east. Recently some of the skeletons originally stolen for university purposes have been repatriated. Most of the skeletons and most looted artifacts have not been recovered. Yet, graves, tombs still exist here. The plows have taken most of the four-hundred-some mounds, once rising six to twenty feet high, down to just over some of the bare bones. Some descendants of this city live within driving distance, yet have no say over the site. Typically they are not invited to interpret their direct history. The City of Sioux Falls is ten minutes away, yet no obvious mention of Blood Run is made in the district's textbooks. The mound city is still evident to those who have understanding of presence. Eighty-some mounds still exist here.

The author hopes that this work will begin to convince the greater populations to come forth and make a stand within their own communities and governments to stop the unnecessary desecration and denial of the remains of extremely valuable civilizations which existed here from coast to coast in pre-contact times; To make fully known the extent of such misportrayal and make amends for such gross wrongdoings; To seek to raise honor and respect for those who built the great cities and villages of Turtle Island and whose direct descendants remarkably still live on today despite the genocidal eras of colonization, industrialization and expansion; To make testimony and recompense to the resilience of Native Peoples today; To hold hope for the future and urge that rightful amends be made to the survivors; To involve the world community in collective preservation of sacred sites.

This volume was written in effort to move the state and its citizens to protect, preserve and honor an Indigenous mound site which was a thriving city of six nations and ten thousand people at the time the first Europeans approached the area now lying across the South Dakota and Iowa borders mere minutes away from Minnesota. The opening poem is a version of the author's oral testimony that urged the State of South Dakota Game Fish & Parks Department to vote unanimously to secure the site after twenty-three years of deliberation. The testimony proved successful in January 2003 at Oacoma, South Dakota. To date, the state has been unable to raise the money necessary to purchase the lands steadily being dwindled away under the plow and by looters. Previous decades of lobbying garnished federal recognition for this site as qualified for National Park Land inclusion. No monies have come from the Federal Government to make it so. The possibility is present . . . A portion of the proceeds from this volume will go to preservation of this site. Additional interest in assisting may be directed to:

<supportfor-bloodrun@yahoo.com>

Dedications

This volume is dedicated to James, Sherwin, Ariruma, Hugo & Aty; I pray we may join our peoples as sisters in the beauty of the world, the truth of memory, and in the wind as it washes us over;

Fernando Rendon, who the whole world surely must honor for creating the phenomenal International Poetry Festival in Medellin, Colombia to provide poems and a place of peace for the people where war exists, and who works tirelessly to bring Indigenous poets together to discuss solution and provide the way. For his dedicated son, his family, and friends; for all the poets and volunteers who find the strength in unity through peace; for Catalina and Juana and all the translators and readers who bring our work to voice;

For the organizers, poets & people of the Venezuela World Poetry Festival; for the Mongrel Jazz players;

For Osvaldo Lopez, Marisa Etselrich, and Alicia Partnoy—for your gifts;

Sherwin Bitsui, Hugo Jamioy, Ariruma Kowii, Gladys Yagari, José Gabriel Alimako, Bienvenido Arroyo, Ramón Gil Barros for the light in the Botanical Gardens of life;

Ramon Palomares, Sujata Bhatt, Alvaro Lasso, Jean-Baptiste Tati-Loutard, Anwar Al-Ghassani, Ali Al-Shalah, Shuntaro Tanikawa, Ibrahim Nasrallah, Edwin Thumboo, Malak Mustafá, Shin Kyong, Chiranan Pitpreecha, Meisún Saker Al-Kasimi, Michael Augustin, Ángela García, Alfonso Kijadurías, Rigoberto Paredes, Maria Baranda, Ernesto Cardenal, William Osuna, Enrique Hernández D'Jesús, Estaban Moore, Sam Hamill, Jorge Rivelli Alejandra Mendé, Julio Azzimonti,

Jorge Chaparro, Javier Aduríz, Juan Fernando, Tarek William Saab, Carlos Osorio, Timothy Wangusa, Bernhard Widder, Wole Soyinka, Derek Walcott, Amiri & Amina Baraka, Quincy & Margaret Troupe, Idris Tayeb, Jorge Cocom Pech, Maria Baranda, Maria Magdalena Figuera, Victor Rojas, Omar Velasquez, Yennis Franco, Luis Segundo Renaud, Miguel Mendoza Barreto, Nestor Francia, Jack Hirschman, Leonel Lienlaf Edgar and our great hosts in in Tucupita and everyone who builds poetic mounds in the world for us to revere;

James Stevens, Joy Harjo, Heid Erdrich, Marilyn Lone Hill Meier, Karenne Wood, Roberta Hill, Carolyn Dunn, Al Hunter, Gordon Henry, Evelina Lucero, Maaganiit Noori, Irwin Sharp Fish Sr., Kim Blaeser, the work in our hearts is surely in our hands;

Simon Ortiz, Richard Van Camp, Buffy Sainte Marie, Turtle Gals, Ulali, Walela, Winona LaDuke, Leslie Marmon Silko, Linda Hogan, Ellen Arnold, Susan Gardner, Susan Weinberg, Joseph Bathanti, Debra Marquart, Mary Lawlor, ML Liebler, Steve Dickison, Arthur Sze, Carol Moldaw, Bob Bensen, Phil Young, Susan Bernardin, Charlotte Zoe, Brent Michael Davids, Susan Richardson, Anne Waldman, Anselm Hollo, Jack Collum, Eleni Sikilienos, Patricia Spears Jones, Elinor Nauen, Deb Klebanoff, Diane Glancy, Juan Felipe Herrera, Margarita Luna Robles, Jim Groth, Jon Davis, Katie Knight, Rea and Jan Knight, Susan Gardner, Anna Lee Walters, Jodi Melamed, Peggy Shumaker, Mary Lawlor, Steve Martin, Kate Gale, Janine Pomey Vega, Ann Beatty, for flourishing;

Janet MacAdams, Chris & Jen Hamilton-Emery, for creating new opportunity for the work;

Louise Glück & Alice Walker for offering inspiration in their meaningful works.

South Dakota Game, Fish and Parks Commission; Lance Foster and the Ioway Cultural Center ("Tanji na Che: Recovering the Landscape of the Ioway."); Iowa Historical Society; Augustana College and Adrien

Hannus; the State of Iowa Parks Bureau; South Dakota Magazine; for site access, support, research information and access to archeological logs (maps and field notes included Pettigrew, Starr, Lewis, Orr, and Henning; papers include "The Map, of the Map, of the Map, of the Map: Tracking the Blood Run Archaeological Site," Lueck, Winham, Hannus, Rossum);

Allan Kornblum, Chris Fishbach, Molly Mikolowski, Lauren Snyder for continual support, outstanding execution, and Coffee House genius;

Mom, Dad, Lucy, Nancy, Travis, James, Sherwin, Stephanie, Kim, and Vaughan, Mary, Hazel, Deja for your presence,

For the victims of global warming, of the Tsunami 2004, Hurricane Katrina 2005, for Gatemouth Brown;

All my colleagues, fellows, and students from the Black Earth Arts Institute, MacDowell Colony for Artists, the South Dakota Arts Council, the Sioux Falls School District, Augustana's Center for Western Studies, Kilian College, Hartwick College, Northern Michigan University, Naropa University, the Institute of American Indian Arts, Whidbey Writers Program, Katchemack Bay, Iowa State University, University of South Dakota, South Dakota State University, Black Hills State University;

For all of those along the way, may you be forever drenched peacefully in the beauty of the night and the light of the day and may your work serve purpose in the struggle for peace and justice always;

In memory of Vine Deloria Jr., Bea Medicine, Reuban Snake;

For Neruda, we do still hear you.

For all who work endlessly to partner poetry and peace;

For the Ho-Chunk, Ioway, Kansa Otoe, Osage, Omaha, Quapaw, Ponca, Missouri, Arikira, Dakota, Cheyenne nations and all other Indigenous nations with history in the Blood Run site.

For Dekanahwidah, The Great Peacemaker, for your work and vision!

Additional recommended sites: <www.ibsgwatch.imagedjinn.com/learn/index.htm> <www.indianlandtenure.org> <www.honorearth.com> <www.cr.nps.gov/nagpra/> <www.sacred-sites.org>

<supportfor-bloodrun@yahoo.com>